A+ Alphabet Books

Wild Animals
ABC

An Alphabet Book

by **Michael Dahl**

Consulting Editor: Gail Saunders-Smith, PhD

Capstone
press

Mankato, Minnesota

A is for anteater.

An anteater's snout hides its long sticky tongue. The anteater shoots out its tongue and catches tasty, tiny ants.

B is for bear.

Bears aren't always fierce and growling.
Sometimes they just like to lie around.

3

C is for crocodile.

What a big mouth! Crocodiles have long sharp teeth.
Don't get too close to this croc.

4

D is for dolphin.

A dolphin leaps out of the ocean. Sunlight flashes on its fin. The dolphin takes a quick look around before plunging back in.

E is for elephant.

An elephant has a long nose called a trunk. It comes in handy for grabbing fruit off a tree.

F is for frog.

Frogs have big round eyes for seeing and strong legs for hopping. Frogs hop around streams and swamps.

G is for gorilla.

Gorillas aren't lazy. They just like to relax.
When their tummies are full of leaves,
they lie down to take a nap.

H is for hippopotamus.

A hippo rises from a muddy lake.
Up comes the hippo, opening
its mouth for a gulp of air.

I is for ibis.

Ibis wade in the water, hunting for food.
Their webbed feet feel for frogs and snails.
Ibis snatch up a snack with their beaks.

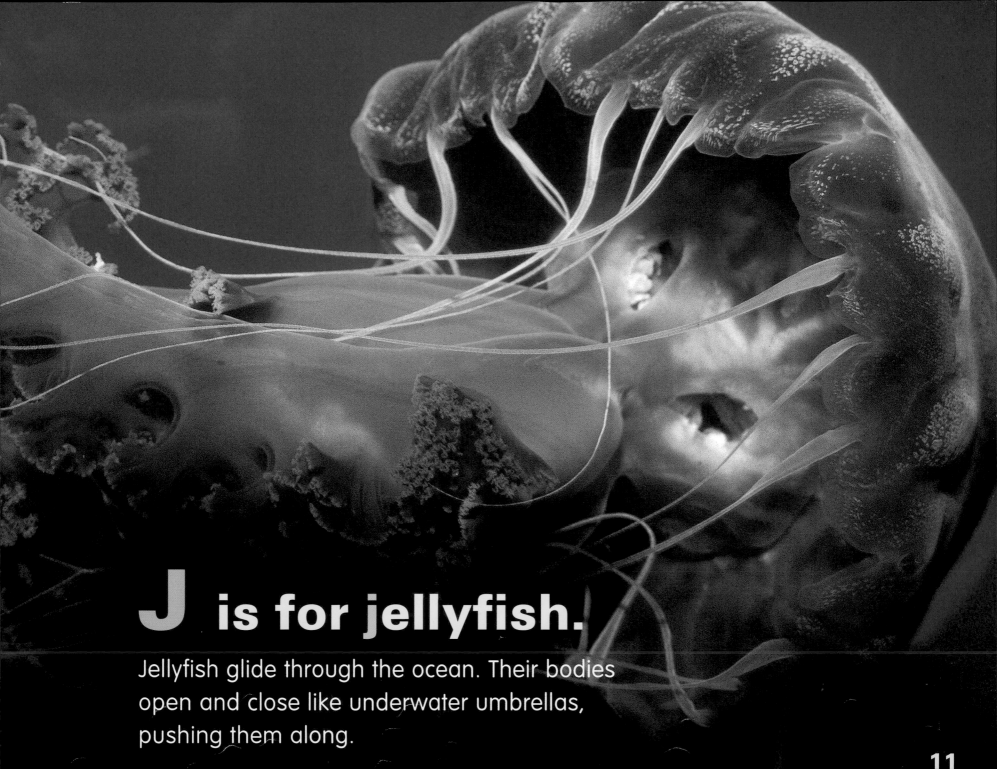

J is for jellyfish.

Jellyfish glide through the ocean. Their bodies open and close like underwater umbrellas, pushing them along.

K is for koala.

Koalas huddle high in the trees.
During the day, they like to sleep.
At night, they nibble on leaves.

12

L is for lion.

The lion is called the king
of beasts. A thick mane of hair
circles its fierce face.

M is for moose.

A moose is on the loose! Moose have huge antlers on their heads. They shed their antlers every winter and grow new antlers in spring.

N is for nutria.

Nutrias live near water. They slip through muddy swamps and nibble on leaves and stems.

O is for octopus.

An eight-armed octopus lives in the ocean. Each wavy arm has rows of suckers. The tiny suckers feel for food that the octopus eats.

P is for penguin.

Penguins waddle on the frozen ground.
Wings help penguins balance as they
wobble around.

17

Q is for quail.

Quail are quiet. When they hear
a strange noise, they sit very still.
They wait for danger to pass.

R is for rhinoceros.

A rhinoceros doesn't like a noisy ruckus. If a rhino is bothered, it lowers its horns and runs.

S is for snake.

A snake can twist and climb. Snakes slither through tall grass. They wrap themselves around branches.

T is for tortoise.

A tortoise moves very slowly. It cannot run for safety. When a tortoise is afraid, it pulls its head and legs inside its hard shell.

U is for sea urchin.

A sea urchin's pointy spines protect it in the ocean. Animals that try to eat urchins get poked.

V is for vampire bat.

A vampire bat always drinks its meals. Beware at night!
Vampires drink the blood of sleeping creatures.

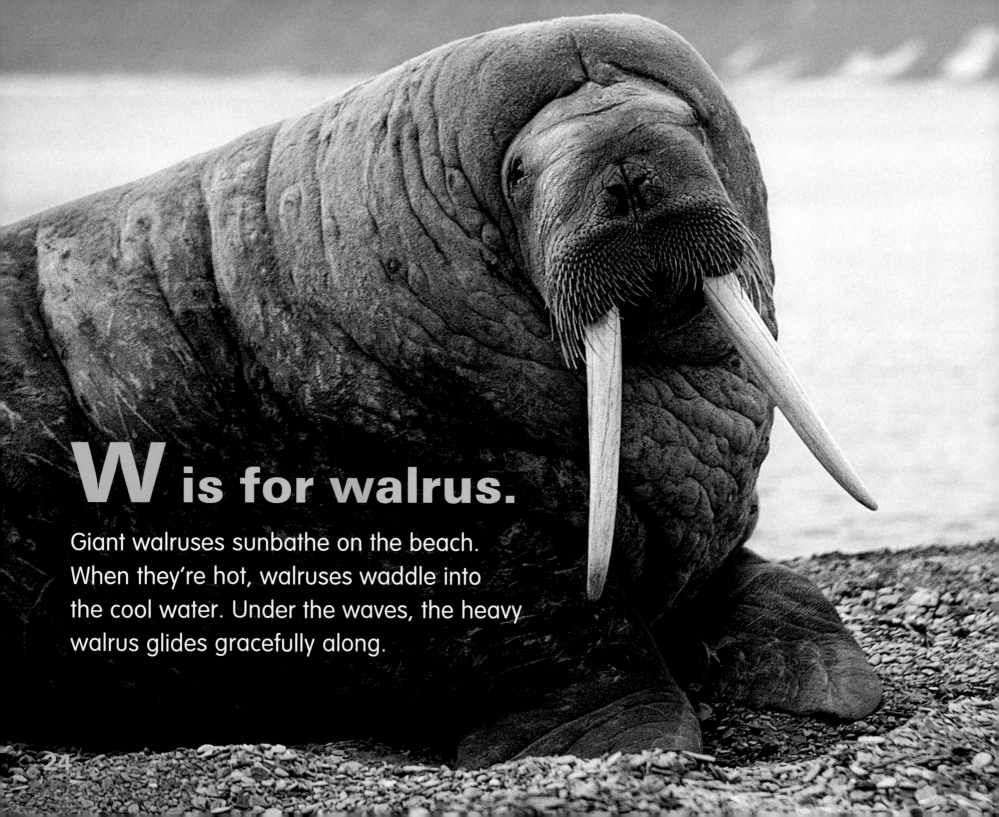

W is for walrus.

Giant walruses sunbathe on the beach. When they're hot, walruses waddle into the cool water. Under the waves, the heavy walrus glides gracefully along.

24

X is for fox.

A fox stops to listen. Its pointed ears catch the softest sound. A fox can hear a mouse squeak from far away.

Y is for yak.

Each summer, yaks shed their shaggy hair. In winter, the hair grows back. Hair keeps yaks warm in the chilly mountain winds.

Z is for zebra.

Zebras hide well in a crowd. It's hard to tell where one zebra ends and another begins.

Fun Facts about Wild Animals

Koalas don't move much. They might stay in the same tree for three or four days.

Elephants can eat up to 500 pounds (227 kilograms) of food a day.

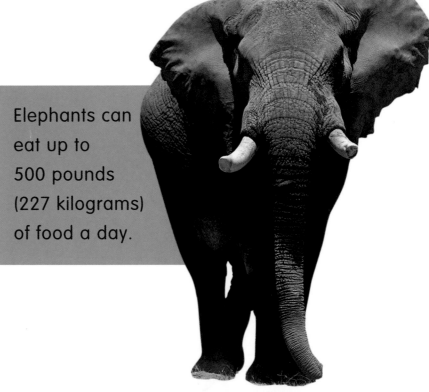

A rhino's horn is made of keratin, the same material that makes up human hair.

Lions are the only wild cats to live in groups. All other wild cats live alone.

Dolphins have no sense of smell.

A male penguin sits on an egg for two months to keep it warm. During this time, the male penguin does not eat. He may lose up to half of his body weight waiting for the chick to hatch.

Walruses have sacs under their throats that they can fill with air. These air sacs help walruses float upright. This way, walruses can sleep in the water without drowning.

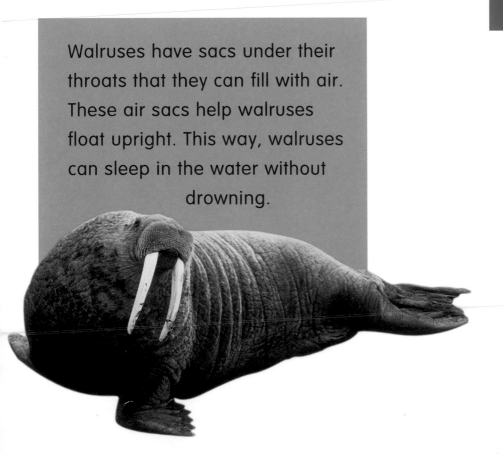

When an octopus is in danger, it squirts out a cloud of black liquid. This "ink" hides the octopus so it can quickly swim away.

Glossary

antler (ANT-lur)—one of the two large bony structures on the head of a moose

fin (FIN)—the part of a dolphin's body that is shaped like a flap; fins help dolphins and fish move through water.

ruckus (RUH-kuhs)—a noisy disturbance

shed (SHED)—to let something fall off; moose shed their antlers; yaks shed their hair.

snout (SNOUT)—the long front part of an animal's head including the nose, mouth, and jaws

spine (SPINE)—a hard, sharp, pointed growth

waddle (WAHD-uhl)—to take short steps while swaying from side to side

wade (WAYD)—to walk through water

Read More

Baker, Leslie. *The Animal ABC.* New York: Henry Holt, 2003.

Butterfield, Moira. *Wild Animals.* Find Out About. North Mankato, Minn.: Chrysalis Education, 2003.

Hammerslough, Jane. *Wild in the U.S.A.* Animal Planet. New York: Scholastic, 2003.

Internet Sites

FactHound offers a safe, fun way to find Internet sites related to this book. All of the sites on FactHound have been researched by our staff.

Here's how:
1. Visit *www.facthound.com*
2. Type in this special code **0736826084** for age-appropriate sites. Or enter a search word related to this book for a more general search.
3. Click on the **Fetch It** button.

FactHound will fetch the best sites for you!

Index

A+ Books are published by Capstone Press
151 Good Counsel Drive, P.O. Box 669, Mankato, Minnesota 56002
www.capstonepress.com

012010
005665R

Library of Congress Cataloging-in-Publication Data
Dahl, Michael.
    Wild animals ABC : an alphabet book / by Michael Dahl.
    p. cm.—(A+ alphabet books)
    Includes bibliographical references and index.
    ISBN-13: 978-0-7368-2608-2 (hardcover)
    ISBN-10: 0-7368-2608-4 (hardcover)
    1. Animals—Juvenile literature. 2. English language—Alphabet—Juvenile literature. I. Title.
QL49.D3132 2005
590—dc22   2004001391

Summary: Introduces wild animals through photographs and brief text that uses one word relating to wild animals for each letter of the alphabet.

Credits
Amanda Doering and June Preszler, editors; Heather Kindseth, designer; Kelly Garvin, photo researcher; Eric Kudalis, product planning editor

Photo Credits
Bruce Coleman Inc./Hans Reinhard, 26; Bruce Coleman Inc./John Shaw, 15, 17, 19; Corbis/Galen Rowell, 25; Corbis/Gavriel Jecan, 21; Corbis/Kennan Ward, 3; Corbis/Renee Lynn, cover; Corbis/Ron Sanford, 14; Corbis/Theo Allofs, 2; Corbis/Yann Arthus-Bertrand, 8; Craig Brandt, 27; DigitalVision/Gerry Ellis, 1, 6, 28 (both), 29 (right); DigitalVision/Joel Simon, 24; Eda Rogers, 11; James P. Rowan, 7, 20; Minden Pictures/Gerry Ellis/Globio, 9; Minden Pictures/Michael & Patricia Fogden, 23; Minden Pictures/Mitsuaki Iwago, 12; Robert McCaw, 10; Ron Kimball Stock/Michael H. Francis, 4; Ron Kimball Stock/Renee Demartin, 5; Ron Kimball Stock/Ron Kimball, 13, 18; Tom Stack & Associates/David B. Fleetham, 16; Tom Stack & Associates/Ed Robinson, 22; U.S. Fish & Wildlife Service/photo by Bill Hickey, 29 (left)

Note to Parents, Teachers, and Librarians
Wild Animals ABC: An Alphabet Book uses colorful photographs and a nonfiction format to introduce children to characteristics about wild animals while building a mastery of the alphabet. This book is designed to be read independently by an early reader or to be read aloud to a pre-reader. The images help early readers and listeners understand the text and concepts discussed. The book encourages further learning by including the following sections: Fun Facts about Wild Animals, Glossary, Read More, Internet Sites, and Index. Early readers may need assistance using these features.